Dealing with Feeling...
Happy

Isabel Thomas

Illustrated by Clare Elsom

Raintree is an imprint of Capstone Global Library Limited, a company incorporated in England and Wales having its registered office at 7 Pilgrim Street, London, EC4V 6LB – Registered company number: 6695582

www.raintreepublishers.co.uk
myorders@raintreepublishers.co.uk

Text © Capstone Global Library Limited 2013
First published in hardback in 2013
Paperback edition first published in 2014
The moral rights of the proprietor have
been asserted.

Edited by Dan Nunn, Rebecca Rissman, and
 Catherine Veitch
Designed by Philippa Jenkins
Original illustrations © Clare Elsom
Illustrated by Clare Elsom
Production by Victoria Fitzgerald
Originated by Capstone Global Library Ltd
Printed and bound in China

ISBN 978 1 406 25039 8 (hardback)
16 15 14 13 12
10 9 8 7 6 5 4 3 2 1

ISBN 978 1 406 25049 7 (paperback)
17 16 15 14
10 9 8 7 6 5 4 3 2 1

British Library Cataloguing in Publication Data
Thomas, Isabel.
Happy. -- (Dealing with Feeling...)
152.4'2-dc23
A full catalogue record for this book is available from the British Library.

Contents

What is happiness? 4

How does it feel to be happy? 6

What makes people happy? 8

What can I do to feel happy? 10

What if I am feeling sad? 12

How can I turn sad feelings into happy ones?.. 14

What is the quickest way to feel happy? 16

What if I have to do something
   I don't like doing? 18

How can I make other people feel happy? 20

Make a happiness toolbox 22

Glossary 23

Find out more 24

Index 24

Some words are shown in bold, **like this.** Find out what they mean in the glossary on page 23.

What is happiness?

happy

jealous

proud

sad

Happiness is a **feeling.**
It is normal to have many
kinds of feelings every day.

Some feelings are nice to have. Happiness is a nice feeling. There are things you can do to feel happy more often.

How does it feel to be happy?

When we are happy, we feel good about ourselves. Smiling or laughing shows other people how we feel.

Being happy makes us feel brave or **confident**. It helps us to do the things that we want to do.

What makes people happy?

Sometimes other people do things to make us happy, such as giving us a surprise present. We can also do things to make ourselves happy.

Many people feel happy if they do well at something. You can make yourself happy by working hard to do well at school and at home.

What can I do to feel happy?

Spending time with other people can make us feel happy. Talking and playing with friends and family is fun.

You can make new friends by smiling and saying "Hello". You can meet new people by playing sport or starting a new **hobby**.

What if I am feeling sad?

Everyone feels sad sometimes. Talking to someone can make you feel happier.

You can make yourself feel happy
by doing something you enjoy.
You could read a book or watch a
funny film.

How can I turn sad feelings into happy ones?

Feelings can change the way that people behave. What do you do when something makes you feel angry, sad, or **jealous**?

If you think happy thoughts it will help you to feel better. If you are cheerful and kind, people will do things to make you happy, too!

What is the quickest way to feel happy?

Try frowning, then smiling. How does it make you feel? You can make yourself feel happier just by smiling!

Smiling makes other people feel friendly towards you, too. Who would you most like to be friends with in this picture?

What if I have to do something I don't like doing?

How do you feel when you are asked to tidy up at school or at home? If someone asks for your help, it means they think you will do a good job.

When you have finished, you will feel **proud**. The person that you helped will be pleased. Helping other people can make YOU feel happy, too!

How can I make other people feel happy?

Nobody feels happy all the time. Your friends and family might feel sad, angry, or worried sometimes.

They might want to talk about how they feel. You can help them to feel happier by listening and by being a good friend.

Make a happiness toolbox

Write down some tips to help you feel happy every day.

Set yourself a goal and work hard to do well at it.

Find a friend or family member to talk to.

Smile!

Read a book or watch a film that you enjoy.

Go for a walk or a run outside.

If you feel sad, try doing something different.

Make someone else happy by helping them.

Learn a new **hobby** or sport.

Don't be afraid to ask for help. Everyone needs help sometimes.

Glossary

confident feeling that you can do something well

feeling something that happens inside our minds. It can affect our bodies and the way we behave.

hobby activity that you do for fun, in your own time

jealous feeling upset or grumpy that you do not have something that another person has

proud feeling pleased with yourself

Find out more

Books

Everybody Feels: Happy, Jane Bingham (QED Publishing, 2006)

Smile a Lot! Nancy Carlson (Lerner, 2012)

You Are My Sunshine, Holly Hobbie (Little, Brown, 2010)

Websites

bbc.co.uk/scotland/education/health/feelings

kidshealth.org/kid/feeling

pbskids.org/arthur/games/aboutface

Index

feeling good 6
giving 8
helping 18, 19
laughing 6
playing 10, 11

smiling 6, 11, 16, 17
talking 10, 12, 21
working hard 9